Design: Jill Coote
Recipe Photography: Peter Barry
Recipe styling: Jacqueline Bellefontaine, Siân Davies,
Bridgeen Deery and Wendy Devenish
Jacket and Illustration Artwork: Jane Winton,
courtesy of Bernard Thornton Artists, London
Compiled and introduced by Laura Potts
Edited by Josephine Bacon

Published by
CHARTWELL BOOKS, INC.
A Division of **BOOK SALES, INC.**
110 Enterprise Avenue
Secaucus, New Jersey 07094
CLB 3355
© 1994 CLB Publishing,
Godalming, Surrey, England
Printed and bound in Singapore

ISBN 1-55521-982-9

THE
LITTLE BOOK
· OF ·

Pasta

RECIPES

A compact, easy-to-follow guide to creating
perfect pasta dishes.

CHARTWELL
BOOKS, INC.

Introduction

*T*he basic recipe for pasta – which at its most simple is literally a *paste* made from flour and water – appears in many cuisines, and takes many forms. It is, however, particularly associated with the Italian and Chinese culinary traditions. The debate as to which of these nations should be credited with its invention has been hotly argued. One thing, however, is certain. Though not unique to Italian cooking, pasta has to a certain extent become synonymous with it.

Pasta comes in a bewildering variety of shapes and sizes. The fundamental reason for this profusion does not lie, as many would believe, in Italian extravagance, or in rivalry between competing dried pasta manufacturers. In fact, different varieties of pasta absorb different amounts of sauce, with some shapes of pasta complementing some sauces better than others. For example, long varieties of dried pasta are best served with oil-based sauces, and generally speaking do not combine well with meat sauces. Rich, creamy sauces and meat sauces, on the other hand, go well with short-cut varieties of pasta, especially those which are hollow, or have grooves where the sauce can be trapped.

Most supermarkets now stock a wide variety of fresh as well as dried pasta. Many people prefer dried pasta for the simple reason that they are more familiar with it and know exactly how to cook it. Like dried pasta, fresh pasta is cooked in boiling, salted water, with a little oil to stop it sticking together. Cooking times for fresh and

dried pasta vary, with dried pasta taking slightly longer. It is essential that pasta is not overcooked, as there is nothing less appetizing than a plateful of limp, soggy spaghetti or tagliatelle. Pasta should be cooked until it is *al dente*, which means tender but firm. There are many ways to test whether pasta is cooked, but the best way is to take a piece and taste it.

Pasta sauces do not have to be elaborate. In fact some of tastiest, most-loved sauces can be prepared very quickly. Melted butter, black pepper, and the lightest sprinkling of freshly-grated Parmesan cheese, for example, or the classic *carbonara* sauce with cream, eggs, and bacon make delicious, easy sauces. The essence of a good pasta sauce lies in the use of fresh ingredients whose flavors enhance each other. Ripe tomatoes, fragrant herbs, black olives, and juicy, sweet peppers are commonly found in pasta sauces.

This book is an invaluable companion to the experienced and inexperienced cook alike. The selection of recipes reflects the versatility of pasta, offering a range of dishes, from those that can be put together very quickly, such as *Tagliatelle with Garlic and Oil*, to the more elaborate baked delights such as *Lasagne* and *Cannelloni*. The step-by-step instructions explain how to create a variety of perfect pasta dishes, highlighting the skills needed to make fresh pasta, and giving ideas for different fillings and sauces.

Minestra

SERVES 4-6

A wholesome soup which makes an ideal starter.

PREPARATION: 15 mins
COOKING: 45 mins

4 ounces short-cut macaroni
2 tbsps olive oil
1 onion
1 carrot
1 stick celery
3 pints water
2 cups fresh spinach
2 tomatoes
1 tsp rosemary
2 tbsps chopped parsley
2 cloves garlic, crushed
4 tbsps Parmesan cheese, grated
Salt and pepper

Step 4 Add the shredded spinach leaves to the soup.

1. Cut onion, carrot, and celery into thick matchstick strips.

2. Heat oil in a large, heavy skillet, and fry vegetable strips until just browning, stirring occasionally.

3. Pour on water, add salt and pepper, and simmer 20 minutes.

4. Meanwhile, wash and cut spinach leaves into shreds, add to soup and cook 10 minutes.

5. Scald and skin tomatoes, and chop roughly, removing seeds.

6. Add tomatoes, macaroni, garlic, parsley, and rosemary to the soup, and simmer a further 10 minutes.

7. Adjust seasoning. Serve with grated Parmesan cheese.

Step 1 Cut onion, carrot, and celery into thick matchstick strips.

Tagliatelle Carbonara

SERVES 4

Bacon, cream, and eggs combine to make a rich pasta sauce.

PREPARATION: 10 mins
COOKING: 15 mins

10 ounces tagliatelle
2 tbsps butter or margarine
4 Canadian bacon slices, chopped
1 tbsp olive oil
4 tbsps single cream
Pinch of paprika
4 tbsps Parmesan cheese, grated
2 eggs
Salt and pepper

Step 4 Beat together eggs and grated cheese.

Step 7 Add bacon mixture and egg mixture, and toss together.

1. Heat the oil in a skillet, and cook the bacon over a moderate heat until just browning.

2. Add the paprika and cook 1 minute.

3. Add the cream, and stir.

4. Beat together the eggs and grated cheese.

5. Cook the tagliatelle in lots of boiling, salted water 10 minutes, or until tender but still firm.

6. Drain the pasta, return to pan with butter and black pepper, and toss.

7. Add bacon mixture and egg mixture, and toss together. Add salt to taste. Serve immediately.

Spaghetti with Tomato, Salami, and Green Olives

SERVES 4

This robust pasta dish is ideal for a quick supper or light lunch.

PREPARATION: 15 mins
COOKING: 15 mins

10 ounces spaghetti
1 x 14-ounce can plum tomatoes
10 slices salami
1 cup green olives, pitted and chopped
1 clove garlic, crushed
2 tbsps olive oil
½ tbsp oregano
4 tbsps grated pecorino cheese
Salt and pepper

Step 2 Add oregano, salami, and olives, and heat gently.

1. Purée tomatoes, and push through a sieve into a saucepan.

2. Add oregano, salami, and olives, and heat gently.

3. Add salt and pepper to taste.

4. Meanwhile, cook spaghetti in plenty of boiling, salted water 10 minutes. Drain well.

5. Heat olive oil, garlic, and freshly-ground black pepper in the pan used to cook the spaghetti.

6. Add spaghetti, and pour the sauce over it. Toss well and serve with pecorino cheese.

Step 1 Purée tomatoes and push through a sieve into a saucepan.

Pasta with Fresh Tomato and Basil Sauce

SERVES 4

Fresh tomato and basil make a classic sauce for pasta.

PREPARATION: 15-20 mins
COOKING: 10-15 mins

---

1 small onion, finely chopped
1 pound fresh tomatoes
2 tbsps tomato paste
1 orange
2 cloves garlic, crushed
Salt and freshly ground black pepper
⅔ cup red wine
⅔ cup chicken broth
2 tbsps coarsely-chopped basil
12 ounces wholewheat pasta

Step 1 To chop an onion finely, pierce the peeled onion with a fork and use this to hold the vegetable steady whilst you chop.

1. Peel and mince the onion.

2. Cut a small cross in the skins of the tomatoes and plunge them into boiling water 30 seconds. Remove and carefully peel away the loosened skin.

3. Cut the tomatoes into quarters, and remove and discard the seeds. Chop the tomato flesh roughly, and put this, the onion, and the tomato paste into a large saucepan.

4. Heat the onion and tomatoes over a gentle heat, stirring continuously until the tomatoes soften and begin to lose their juice.

5. Finely grate the rind from the orange. Cut the orange in half and squeeze out the juice.

6. Put the orange rind and juice into a large saucepan along with all the remaining ingredients, and bring to the boil.

7. Continue to boil until the sauce has reduced and thickened and the vegetables are soft.

8. Whilst the sauce is cooking, put the pasta into another saucepan with enough boiling water to cover. Season with a little salt and cook 10-15 minutes, or until the pasta is soft.

9. Drain the pasta in a colander, and stir it into the hot sauce. Serve at once with a salad.

Tagliatelle with Garlic and Oil

SERVES 4

Garlic and oil combine to make the simplest of pasta sauces.

PREPARATION: 5 mins
COOKING: 10 mins

10 ounces green tagliatelle
⅔ cup olive oil
3 cloves garlic, crushed
2 tbsps chopped parsley
Salt and pepper

Step 5 Toss the tagliatelle in the sauce to coat well.

Step 5 Add sauce to tagliatelle.

1. Cook the tagliatelle in lots of boiling, salted water 10 minutes, or until tender but still firm, stirring occasionally.

2. Meanwhile, heat the oil in a skillet and, when warm, add peeled, crushed garlic.

3. Fry gently until golden-brown.

4. Add chopped parsley, and salt and pepper to taste.

5. Drain tagliatelle. Add sauce, and toss to coat well. Serve hot.

Home-made Tagliatelle with Summer Sauce

SERVES 4

Home-made pasta is in a class by itself.

PREPARATION: 30 mins
COOKING: 5-6 mins

Pasta Dough
1 cup all-purpose flour
1 cup fine farina (Cream of Wheat)
2 large eggs
2 tsps olive oil
Pinch salt

Sauce
1 pound unpeeled tomatoes, seeded, and cut
　into small dice
1 large green bell pepper, cored, seeded, and
　cut in small dice
1 onion, cut in small dice
1 tbsp chopped fresh basil
1 tbsp chopped fresh parsley
2 cloves garlic, crushed
⅔ cup olive oil and vegetable oil mixed

1. Place the flour and farina in a mound on a
work surface and make a well in the center.
Place the eggs, oil, and salt in the center of the
well.

2. Using a fork, beat the ingredients in the
center to blend them and gradually incorporate
the flour from the outside edge.

3. When half the flour is incorporated, start

Step 4 Roll the
dough out
thinly and cut
into thin strips.

kneading, using the palms of the hands and not
the fingers. Cover the dough and leave it to rest
15 minutes.

4. Divide the dough into quarters and roll out
thinly with a rolling-pin on a floured surface or
use a pasta machine, dusting dough lightly with
flour before rolling. Allow the sheets of pasta to
dry about 10 minutes on a floured surface. Cut
the sheets into strips about ¼ inch wide by
hand or machine, dusting lightly with flour
while cutting. Leave the cut pasta to dry while
preparing the sauce.

5. Combine all the sauce ingredients, mixing
well. Cover and refrigerate overnight.

6. Cook the pasta 5-6 minutes in boiling, salted
water with a spoonful of oil. Drain the pasta
and rinse under very hot water. Toss in a
colander to drain excess water. Place in a
serving dish and coat with the cold sauce.

Penne with Ham and Asparagus

SERVES 4

The Italian word penne means quills, due to the diagonal cut on both ends.

PREPARATION: 20 mins
COOKING: 10 mins

8 ounces penne
12 ounces fresh asparagus
4 ounces cooked ham
2 tbsps butter or margarine
1¼ cup heavy cream
4 tbsps grated Parmesan cheese (optional)

1. Using a swivel vegetable peeler, scrape the sides of the asparagus spears starting about 2 inches from the top. Cut off the ends of the spears about 1 inch from the bottom.

2. Cut the ham into strips about ½ inch thick.

3. Bring a sauté pan of salted water to the boil. Move the pan so it is half on and half off direct

Step 1 Peel the asparagus stalks with a swivel vegetable peeler.

Step 4 Cut ham and cooked asparagus into 1-inch lengths. Leave the asparagus tips whole.

heat. Place in the asparagus spears so that the tips are off the heat. Cover and bring back to the boil. Cook the asparagus spears about 2 minutes. Drain and allow to cool.

4. Cut the asparagus into 1 inch lengths, leaving the tips whole.

5. Melt the butter in the sauté pan and add the asparagus and ham. Cook briefly to evaporate the liquid, and add the cream. Bring to the boil and cook about 5 minutes to thicken the cream.

6. Meanwhile, cook the pasta in boiling, salted water with a little oil for about 10-12 minutes.

7. Drain the pasta and rinse under hot water. Toss in a colander to drain and mix with the sauce. Serve with grated Parmesan cheese, if desired.

Spaghetti Amatriciana

SERVES 4

Chili pepper brings a fiery taste to this pasta sauce.

PREPARATION: 20-25 mins
COOKING: 10-12 mins

1 onion
6 slices smoked bacon
1 pound ripe tomatoes
1 red chili pepper
1½ tbsps oil
12 ounces spaghetti

Step 4 Remove the stem, seeds, and core from the chili pepper, cut into thin strips and then chop into fine dice.

1. Slice the onion thinly. Remove rind from the bacon and cut into thin strips.

2. Drop the tomatoes into boiling water for 6-8 seconds. Remove and place in cold water, and leave to cool. This will make the peels easier to remove.

3. When the tomatoes are peeled, cut them in half and remove the seeds and pulp with a teaspoon. Chop the tomato flesh roughly and set it aside.

4. Cut the chili pepper in half lengthwise. Remove the seeds and core, and cut the pepper into thin strips. Cut the strips into small dice.

5. Heat the oil in a sauté pan and add the onion and bacon. Stir over medium heat about 5 minutes, until the onion is transparent. Drain off excess fat and add the tomatoes and chili. Mix well. Simmer the sauce gently, uncovered, about 5 minutes, stirring occasionally.

6. Meanwhile, cook the spaghetti in boiling, salted water with a little oil about 10-12 minutes. Drain and rinse in hot water and toss in a colander to dry. To serve, spoon the sauce on top of the spaghetti, and sprinkle with freshly-grated Parmesan cheese.

Step 2 Placing tomatoes in boiling water and then in cold water makes the skins easier to remove.

Spirali with Spinach and Bacon

SERVES 4

*Pasta doesn't have to have a sauce that cooks for hours.
This whole dish takes about 20 minutes. True Italian "fast food"!*

PREPARATION: 10 mins
COOKING: 10 mins

12 ounces pasta spirals
2 cups fresh spinach
3 slices bacon
1 clove garlic, crushed
1 small red or green chili pepper
1 small red sweet pepper
1 small onion
3 tbsps olive oil
Salt and pepper

1. Cook the pasta in boiling, salted water about 10-12 minutes or until just tender. Drain in a colander and rinse. Keep the pasta in a bowl of water until ready to use.

Step 2 Tear stalks off the spinach and wash the leaves well.

Step 4 Roll up the leaves in several layers to shred them faster.

2. Tear the stalks off the spinach and wash the leaves well, changing the water several times. Set aside to drain.

3. Remove the rind from the bacon and dice the bacon finely. Cut the chili and the red pepper in half, remove the stems, core and seeds, and slice finely. Slice the onion thinly.

4. Shred the spinach finely.

5. Heat the oil in a sauté pan and add garlic, onion, peppers, and bacon. Fry 2 minutes, add the spinach and fry a further 2 minutes, stirring continuously. Season with salt and pepper.

6. Drain the pasta spirals and toss them in a colander to remove excess water. Mix with the spinach sauce and serve immediately.

Gianfottere Salad

SERVES 4

This delicious Italian salad makes the most of summer vegetables.

PREPARATION: 30 mins
COOKING: 30 mins

1 small eggplant
2 tomatoes
1 large zucchini
1 red bell pepper
1 green bell pepper
1 medium onion
1 clove garlic, peeled
4 tbsps olive oil
Salt and pepper
1 pound wholewheat pasta spirals

1. Cut the eggplant into ½-inch slices. Sprinkle with salt and leave 30 minutes.

2. Chop the tomatoes roughly and remove the cores.

3. Cut the zucchini into ½-inch slices.

Step 1 Cut the eggplant into ½-inch slices and sprinkle with plenty of salt.

Step 8 Add the eggplant, zucchini, peppers, tomatoes, and garlic to the onion in the skillet.

4. Core and seed the peppers, and chop them rough

5. Chop the onion. Crush the garlic.

6. Heat 3 tbsps olive oil in a skillet, and sauté the onion gently, until it is transparent.

7. Rinse the salt from the eggplant and pat dry. Chop the eggplant roughly.

8. Stir the eggplant, zucchini, peppers, tomatoes, and garlic into the onion, and fry gently 20 minutes. Season to taste, and allow to cool completely.

9. Cook the pasta spirals in plenty of boiling, salted water for 10-15 minutes.

10. Rinse the pasta in cold water and drain well.

11. Put the pasta into a large mixing bowl, and stir in the remaining olive oil.

12. Stir in the vegetables, mixing well.

Tuna and Tomato Salad

SERVES 4

Serve this salad as part of a summer lunch with a green salad and French bread.

PREPARATION: 10 mins
COOKING: 15 mins

---

1 tbsp chopped fresh basil or marjoram
6 tbsps French dressing
12 ounces pasta spirals
6 tomatoes
1½ cups canned tuna, drained

---

1. Mix the basil or marjoram, with the French dressing.

2. Cook the pasta in a large saucepan of boiling, lightly salted water about 10 minutes.

3. Rinse in cold water and drain well, shaking off any excess water.

4. Put the pasta into a large bowl and toss with

Step 7 Add the tuna to the pasta and mix together gently.

3 tablespoons of the French dressing, mixing well to ensure that they are evenly coated. Leave to cool.

5. Slice enough of the tomatoes to arrange around the outside of the serving dish and then chop the rest.

6. Put the chopped tomatoes into another bowl and pour the remaining French dressing over them. Arrange this in the center of a serving dish.

7. Add the flaked tuna to the pasta and toss together gently.

8. Pile the pasta and tuna over the chopped tomatoes in the center of the dish.

9. Arrange the tomato slices around the edge of the serving dish, and chill well until required.

Step 4 Mix the pasta spirals with 3 tbsps of the French dressing in a large bowl.

Mushroom Pasta Salad

SERVES 4

The piquant lemon marinade brings zest to this easy salad.

PREPARATION: 10 mins, plus 1 hr to marinate the
   mushrooms
COOKING: 15 mins

---

5 tbsps olive oil
Juice of 2 lemons
1 tsp fresh chopped basil
1 tsp fresh chopped parsley
Salt and pepper
2 cups mushrooms
8 ounces wholewheat pasta shapes

---

1. Mix together the olive oil, lemon juice, herbs, and seasoning.

Step 2 Use a sharp knife to slice the mushrooms thinly.

Step 6 Stir the cooled pasta into the marinated mushrooms, mixing well to coat evenly.

2. Finely slice the mushrooms and add these to the lemon dressing in the bowl, stirring well.

3. Cover the bowl and allow to stand in a cool place for at least 1 hour.

4. Cook the pasta in boiling, salted water 10-15 minutes.

5. Rinse the pasta in cold water and drain well.

6. Add the pasta to the marinated mushrooms and lemon dressing, mixing well to coat evenly.

7. Adjust the seasoning if necessary, then chill well before serving.

Macaroni Cheese with Frankfurters

SERVES 4
A hearty family supper dish, ideal for cold winter evenings.

8 frankfurters or wieners
1 pound macaroni
4 tbsps butter or margarine
¾ cup all-purpose flour
2¼ cups milk
¾ cup grated yellow cheese
1 tsp dry mustard powder
Salt and pepper

1. Poach the sausages 5-6 minutes in slightly salted, boiling water.

2. Remove the skins from the sausages and, when cold, slice diagonally.

3. Cook the macaroni in plenty of boiling, salted water for about 10-15 minutes.

Step 2 Remove the skins from the sausages and cut them diagonally into slices about 1 inch long.

Step 6 Add the milk gradually, beating the mixture well between additions, until all the milk is incorporated.

4. Rinse in cold water and drain well.

5. Melt the butter in a saucepan. Stir in the flour and cook 1 minute.

6. Remove the pan from the heat and add the milk gradually, beating thoroughly and returning the pan to the heat to cook between additions. When all the milk has been added, simmer 2 minutes, stirring occasionally.

7. Stir in the sausages, grated cheese, and mustard. Season to taste.

8. Add the drained macaroni to the sauce and stir well until heated through.

9. Pour the mixture into an ovenproof dish and sprinkle the top with a little extra grated cheese.

10. Cook under a preheated, moderate broiler, until the top is golden-brown.

Lasagne Rolls

SERVES 4

An interesting way of using sheets of lasagne.

PREPARATION: 10 mins
COOKING: 15 mins

---

8 lasagne sheets
½ cup button mushrooms, sliced
8 ounces skinned and boned chicken breast
2 tbsps butter or margarine
2 tbsps all-purpose flour
⅔ cup milk
⅔ cup yellow or Swiss cheese, grated
Salt and pepper

Step 11 Spread the chicken mixture evenly over each sheet of lasagne and roll up like a jellyroll.

1. Fill a large saucepan two-thirds full with salted water. Add a little oil and bring to the boil.

2. Add 1 sheet of lasagne, wait about 2 minutes, then add another sheet. Cook only a few at a time and after about 6-7 minutes remove and rinse under cold water. Allow to drain.

3. Repeat this process until all the lasagne are cooked.

4. Wash and slice the mushrooms; slice the chicken breast into thin strips.

5. Melt half the butter in a small skillet and sauté the mushrooms and the chicken.

6. In a small saucepan, melt the rest of the butter. Stir in the flour and cook one minute.

7. Remove the pan from the heat and add the milk gradually, stirring well and returning the pan to the heat between additions, to thicken the sauce.

8. Beat the sauce well and cook 3 minutes.

9. Pour the sauce into the skillet with the chicken and the mushrooms. Add half the cheese and mix well. Season to taste.

10. Lay the sheets of lasagne on a board and divide the chicken mixture equally between them.

11. Spread the chicken mixture evenly over each lasagne sheet and roll up lengthwise, jellyroll fashion.

12. Put the rolls into an ovenproof dish. Sprinkle with the remaining cheese and broil under a pre-heated moderate broiler, until the cheese is bubbly and golden-brown.

Lasagne Napoletana

SERVES 6

This is lasagne as it is cooked and eaten in Naples.

PREPARATION: 25 mins
COOKING: 1-1¼hrs

---

9 sheets spinach lasagne

Tomato Sauce
3 tbsps olive oil
2 cloves garlic, crushed
2 cups canned tomatoes, drained
2 tbsps chopped fresh basil, six whole leaves
    reserved
Salt and pepper
Pinch sugar

Cheese Filling
1 pound ricotta cheese
4 tbsps unsalted butter
2 cups grated Mozzarella cheese
Salt and pepper
Pinch nutmeg

---

1. Cook the pasta 8 minutes in boiling, salted water with a little oil. Drain and rinse under hot water and place in a single layer on a damp cloth. Cover with another damp cloth and set aside.

2. To prepare the sauce, cook the garlic in remaining oil about 1 minute in a large saucepan. When pale brown, add the tomatoes, basil, salt, pepper, and sugar.

Step 5 Place pasta on the base of an oiled baking dish. Spread tomato sauce over.

3. Lower the heat under the saucepan and simmer the sauce 35 minutes. Add more seasoning or sugar to taste.

4. Beat the ricotta cheese and butter together until creamy and stir into the remaining ingredients.

5. Place 3 sheets of lasagne in a greased baking dish. Cover with one third of the sauce and carefully spread with a layer of cheese. Place another 3 layers of pasta over the cheese and cover with another third of the sauce. Add the remaining cheese filling and cover with the remaining pasta. Spoon the remaining sauce on top.

6. Cover with foil and bake 20 minutes in a preheated 375° oven. Uncover and cook 10 minutes longer. Garnish with the reserved leaves and leave to stand 10-15 minutes before serving.

Fish Ravioli

SERVES 4

This ravioli dish is served with a subtly flavored cream-and-lemon sauce.

PREPARATION: 30 mins
COOKING: 30 mins

Dough
1 cup all-purpose flour
3 eggs

8 ounces sole fillets
2 tbsps breadcrumbs
2 eggs, beaten
1 green onion (scallion), finely chopped
1 slice onion
1 slice lemon
6 peppercorns
1 bayleaf
1 tbsp lemon juice
1¼ cups water

Lemon sauce
2 tbsps butter or margarine
2 tbsps flour
2 tbsps double cream
2 tbsps lemon juice

1. Pre-heat oven to 350°F. Place fish in ovenproof dish with onion, lemon, peppercorns, bayleaf, lemon juice, and water. Cover and cook 20 minutes.

2. Remove fish from liquid, and allow to drain. Strain liquid, and set aside.

3. When fish is cool, beat to a pulp. Add the eggs,

Step 6 Shape the filling into small balls, and set them about 1½ inches apart on one half of the dough.

breadcrumbs, and green onion, and season.

4. Sift flour into a bowl and add the eggs. Work together with a spoon, then knead by hand until smooth. Leave 15 minutes.

5. Lightly flour a board, and roll out dough thinly into a rectangle. Cut dough in half.

6. Shape the filling into small balls, and set them about 1½ inches apart on one half of the dough. Place the other half on top, and cut with a ravioli cutter. Seal the edges.

7. Cook in batches in boiling, salted water about 8 minutes, then drain.

8. To make the sauce, melt the butter in a pan, then stir in flour. Remove from the heat, and gradually stir in the liquid from cooked fish. Return to the heat and bring to the boil. Simmer, add the cream, and mix well. Season.

9. Remove from the heat, and gradually stir in the lemon juice. Do not reboil. Pour the sauce over the ravioli and serve.

Cannelloni

SERVES 4

This tasty meat dish justifiably remains a favorite.

PREPARATION: 10 mins
COOKING: 1 hr

---

12 cannelloni shells
2 tbsps Parmesan cheese, grated

1 pound ground lean beef
1 tbsp olive oil
1 onion, peeled and chopped
2 cloves garlic, crushed
1 x 8 ounce package frozen spinach, thawed
½ tsp oregano
1 tsp tomato paste
4 tbsps cream
1 egg, lightly beaten

Tomato sauce
1 tbsp olive oil
1 onion, peeled and chopped
1 clove garlic, crushed
1 x 14-ounce can plum tomatoes
2 tbsps tomato paste

White sauce
1¼ cup milk
2 tbsps butter or margarine
2 tbsps flour

---

1. Heat the oil in a skillet, and fry garlic and onion gently until soft and transparent.

2. Add meat and cook until well browned. Add

Step 4
Carefully fill the cannelloni with the meat mixture.

tomato paste and oregano, and cook gently 15 minutes.

3. Add spinach, egg, cream, and salt and pepper to taste.

4. Cook pasta in boiling, salted water for 15-20 minutes. Rinse and drain. Fill with meat mixture.

5. To make the tomato sauce, heat the oil in a pan, add onion and garlic, and cook gently until transparent. Add tomatoes and tomato paste, and season to taste. Bring to boil, and then simmer for 5 minutes. Set aside.

6. To make the white sauce, melt the butter in the pan. Remove from heat and stir in flour. Gradually add milk, and bring to the boil, stirring continuously, until sauce thickens. Add seasoning.

7. Spread tomato sauce in an ovenproof dish. Lay the pasta on top, and cover with white sauce. Sprinkle with Parmesan cheese, and bake in a preheated 350°F oven 30 minutes.

Spinach Lasagne

SERVES 4

Spinach flavored with nutmeg makes a delicious filling for lasagne.

PREPARATION: 10 mins
COOKING: 30 mins

8 sheets green lasagne

Spinach sauce
6 tbsps butter or margarine
1½ cups frozen spinach, thawed and chopped
   finely
Pinch of ground nutmeg
6 tbsps flour
⅔ cup milk
Salt and pepper

Mornay sauce
2 tbsps butter or margarine
2 tbsps flour
⅔ cup milk
6 tbsps Parmesan cheese, grated
1 tsp French mustard
Salt

1. To make spinach sauce, heat butter in pan, stir in flour, and cook 30 seconds.

2. Remove from heat and stir in milk gradually.

3. Return to heat, and bring to the boil, stirring continuously. Cook 3 minutes.

4. Add spinach, nutmeg, and salt and pepper to taste. Set aside.

Step 9 Line the base with a layer of lasagne, followed by some of the spinach mixture and a layer of cheese sauce.

5. Cook spinach lasagne in lots of boiling, salted water for 10 minutes. Rinse in cold water and drain carefully. Dry on a clean cloth.

6. To make Mornay sauce, heat butter in a saucepan and stir in flour, cooking 30 seconds.

7. Remove from heat, and stir in milk. Return to heat, stirring continuously, until boiling. Continue stirring, and simmer 3 minutes.

8. Remove from heat, and add mustard, two-thirds of cheese, and salt to taste.

9. Grease an ovenproof baking dish. Line the base with a layer of lasagne, followed by some of the spinach mixture, and a layer of cheese sauce.

10. Repeat the process, finishing with a layer of lasagne with a covering of cheese sauce.

11. Sprinkle with the remaining cheese. Bake in a preheated 400°F oven until golden on top. Serve immediately.

Index

Spaghetti with Tomato, Salami and Green Olives